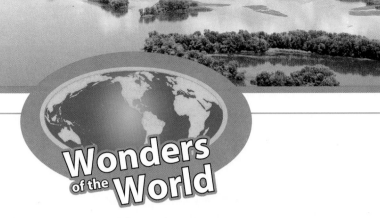

Wonders of the World

Mississippi River

North America's Largest River

Janeen R. Adil

www.av2books.com

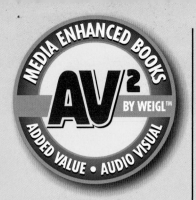

AV² provides enriched content that supplements and complements this book. Weigl's AV² books strive to create inspired learning and engage young minds in a total learning experience.

Your AV² Media Enhanced books come alive with...

 Audio
Listen to sections of the book read aloud.

 Key Words
Study vocabulary, and complete a matching word activity.

 Video
Watch informative video clips.

 Quizzes
Test your knowledge.

Go to **www.av2books.com**, and enter this book's unique code.

 Embedded Weblinks
Gain additional information for research.

 Slide Show
View images and captions, and prepare a presentation.

BOOK CODE

L702746

 Try This!
Complete activities and hands-on experiments.

... and much, much more!

AV² by Weigl brings you media enhanced books that support active learning.

Published by AV² by Weigl
350 5th Avenue, 59th Floor
New York, NY 10118
Website: www.av2books.com   www.weigl.com

Library of Congress Cataloging-in-Publication Data

Adil, Janeen R.
Mississippi river / Janeen R. Adil.
     p. cm. -- (Wonders of the world)
Includes index.
ISBN 978-1-62127-475-9 (hardcover : alk. paper) -- ISBN 978-1-62127-481-0 (softcover : alk. paper)
  1. Mississippi River--Juvenile literature. I. Title.
F351.A35 2013
977--dc23
                         2012040451

Printed in the United States of America in North Mankato, Minnesota
1 2 3 4 5 6 7 8 9 17 16 15 14 13 12

122012
WEP301112

Editor Heather Kissock
Design Mandy Christiansen

Every reasonable effort has been made to trace ownership and to obtain permission to reprint copyright material. The publishers would be pleased to have any errors or omissions brought to their attention so that they may be corrected in subsequent printings.

Photo Credits
Weigl acknowledges Getty Images as its primary photo supplier for this title.

Contents

The Mighty Mississippi

The Mississippi River is the largest river in North America. It supplies water to millions of people. People and wildlife need the river for drinking water, and farmers use it to water their crops. No wonder this river is often called the Mighty Mississippi.

On a map, the Mississippi River appears to divide the United States. The river has actually brought the country together. Before there were cars and trains, the Mississippi River was a major transportation route. Settlers used canoes to travel to new parts of the land. American Indians, and later the Europeans, settled along its banks.

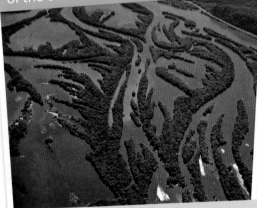

The Mississippi River basin drains 41 percent of the continental United States.

Many bridges have been built across the Mississippi. One of the best known is the Horace Wilkinson Bridge in Baton Rouge, Louisiana.

Mississippi River Facts

- The Mississippi River is 2,350 miles (3,782 kilometers) long. That is as long as 322,000 school buses parked end to end.

- The Mississippi River borders 10 states.

- Streams and rivers from 31 states drain into the Mississippi River.

- The Mississippi River's **basin** makes up 40 percent of the land in the United States.

- About 12 million people live along the Mississippi River.

- Every second, 612,000 cubic feet (17,330 cubic meters) of water is discharged from the Mississippi River into the Gulf of Mexico.

Map of the Mississippi River

CANADA

UNITED STATES

Minnesota

Wisconsin

Iowa

Illinois

Missouri

Kentucky

Tennessee

Arkansas

Mississippi

Louisiana

GULF OF MEXICO

LEGEND

Water

Mississippi River

State Borders

International Borders

N

0 — 250 miles

0 — 250 km

Pelicans are just one type of bird that lives around the Mississippi River.

The American lotus thrives in the quiet backwaters of the Mississippi. The plant can live in water up to 8 feet (2.4 m) deep.

Where in the World?

The Mississippi River is divided into three parts. The Upper Mississippi runs from Lake Itasca, Minnesota to St. Louis, Missouri. The river begins as a stream small enough to step over. Its size increases as it heads south.

The trumpeter swan is common along the Mississippi River. Its wingspan can be up to 8 feet (2.4 m), making it the largest of all swans.

The Middle Mississippi begins at St. Louis, where the Mississippi and Missouri Rivers meet. It continues to Cairo, Illinois, where it meets the Ohio River. At this point, the river becomes the Lower Mississippi. This part of the river flows southward through the states of Illinois, Missouri, Kentucky, Tennessee, Arkansas, Mississippi, and Louisiana before draining into the Gulf of Mexico.

At the Mississippi River's source, the average surface speed of the water is just 1.2 miles (1.9 km) per hour. By comparison, most people walk at a speed of 3 miles (4.8 km) per hour.

Puzzler

The Mississippi River is one of the most important bodies of water in the United States.

Q. What are some of the other major rivers of the United States?

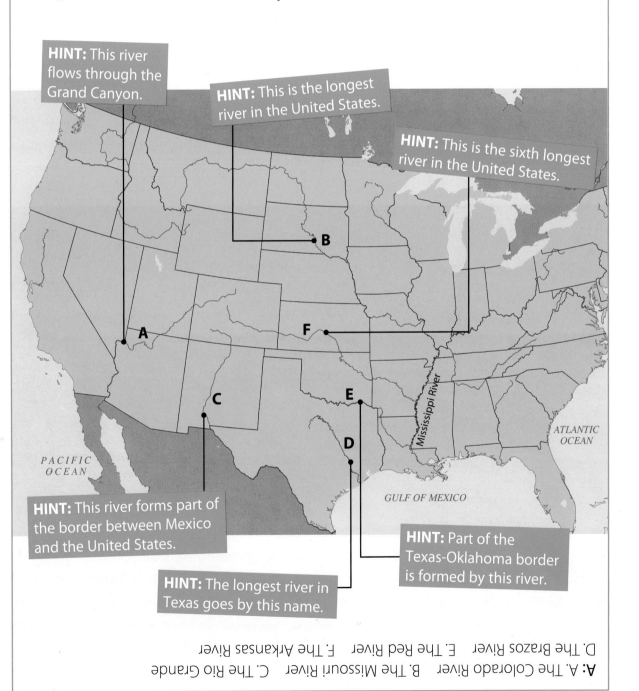

HINT: This river flows through the Grand Canyon.

HINT: This is the longest river in the United States.

HINT: This is the sixth longest river in the United States.

HINT: This river forms part of the border between Mexico and the United States.

HINT: The longest river in Texas goes by this name.

HINT: Part of the Texas-Oklahoma border is formed by this river.

A: A. The Colorado River   B. The Missouri River   C. The Rio Grande
D. The Brazos River   E. The Red River   F. The Arkansas River

A Trip Back in Time

Nearly 2 million years ago, **glaciers** covered parts of North America. Their movement was a major force in shaping the Mississippi River. These gigantic ice sheets were at least 1 mile (1.6 km) thick. The Wisconsin glacier was the last of the great glaciers in North America.

About 10,000 to 12,000 years ago, the Wisconsin glacier shrank toward the north. Its movement carved out parts of the Mississippi riverbed. The melting glacier also left large amounts of water, which formed the Mississippi River as well as streams and lakes. The glacier also wore away rocks and left sediment behind. The changing landscape continued to alter the Mississippi River's shape.

When glaciers move, they often leave scratches or gouges in the rock beneath them. These scratches, called glacial grooves, can be used by scientists to determine the direction of glacier movement.

Anatomy of a River

What has branches, a trunk, and roots? A tree—and a river! A river also has parts called branches, trunk, and roots. A river's branches, trunk, and roots are different from those of a tree.

Branches: Branches flowing into a river are called **tributaries**. As these streams flow into a river, they bring water and **sediment**. The Missouri River is a major tributary to the Mississippi River.

Trunk: A river's trunk is its main channel. Water and sediment move along the river's channel to the ocean.

Roots: A river's roots are the streams that empty into its **delta**. Here, sediment and water flow into the ocean. Sediment is also left behind in the delta. The Mississippi Delta is an area of rich, flat land where cotton, rice, and soybeans are grown.

Water at Work

Water is the most precious resource on Earth. All living things depend on it. Earth is covered by more water than land. About 97 percent of Earth's water is salt water in the oceans. The remaining 3 percent is fresh water. However, two-thirds of the fresh water is frozen in glaciers and ice caps. Only about one-third of the 3 percent is available for use by people and land animals.

Earth recycles its water. This means that humans are using the same water that dinosaurs did. The **water cycle** describes the way water moves above, on, and below the ground. The cycle has four stages.

Stages of the Water Cycle

Storage
Water can be stored in the ground and in oceans, lakes, and rivers. It can also be stored in glaciers and ice caps.

Evaporation
When water evaporates, it changes from a liquid to a gas, or vapor. Heat makes water evaporate more quickly.

Precipitation
Water vapor collects in clouds. It then falls to the ground as precipitation, such as rain or snow. Every day, precipitation is falling somewhere in the world.

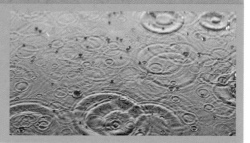

Runoff
Runoff is precipitation that flows into rivers and streams. The water reaches them by flowing either on or through the ground. Heavy rains result in runoff. Floods may occur when a river cannot hold all of this water.

The Water Cycle

The Mississippi River is part of the water cycle. Because it is a river, water is stored in the Mississippi. Water also evaporates from the river, forming clouds. When the clouds cannot hold more moisture, precipitation falls from them, entering the Mississippi River once again. Finally, when the Mississippi River becomes too full, water runoff may cause flooding.

The illustration below shows how the Mississippi River is part of the water cycle.

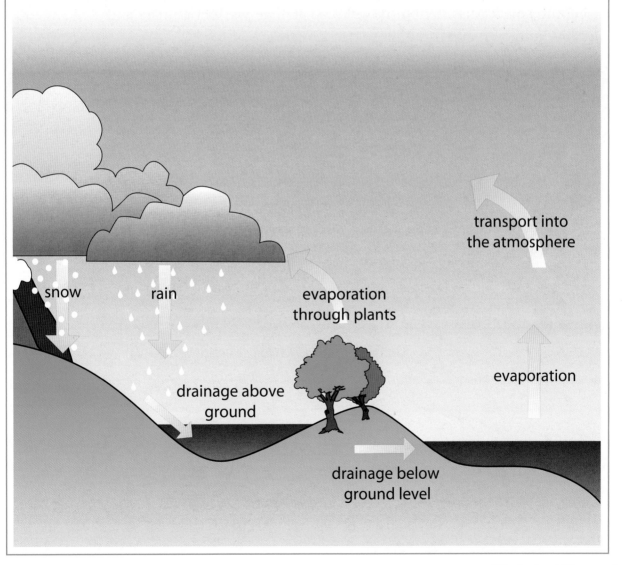

transport into
the atmosphere

snow   rain   evaporation
                       through plants

                                        evaporation

        drainage above
            ground

              drainage below
              ground level

Life along the River

More than 400 **species** of wildlife live along or in the Mississippi River. Each section of the river has its own species and habitats.

In the north, pine and spruce forests line the **headwaters**. This is where bear, elk, moose, and wolves make their homes. Overhead, eagles and snowy owls soar over beds of wild rice.

The Upper Mississippi includes many different habitats. Among them are lakes, marshes, forests, and beaches. Part of this area is protected as a national **refuge**.

Along the Lower Mississippi, the land is flat. The warmer climate and plentiful rainfall make this a more tropical area.

During the winter, up to 2,500 bald eagles live along the Mississippi River. Bald eagles use their sharp talons to catch fish.

River Ecosystems

The Mississippi River coastal wetlands are disappearing at a rate of 25 square miles (65 sq. km) per year. Wetlands are an important ecosystem because they are home to a wide variety of plant and animal life. They also help control floods and protect shorelines.

A special type of **ecosystem** occurs where the Lower Mississippi drains into the Gulf of Mexico. This is an area of coastal **wetlands**, where fresh water and salt water meet.

These wetlands are home to fish, crabs, shrimp, oysters, shore birds, and many other animals. Cypress trees drip with Spanish moss. Mangrove trees sink their roots into the water. Many alligators live in the saltwater marshes.

Early Explorers

The first European to see the Mississippi River was Hernando de Soto, in 1541. He left Spain in search of gold. De Soto and his 600-person crew explored southeastern Florida without finding gold. Soon after crossing the Mississippi River, de Soto died and was buried in the river.

Other early explorers came from France. In 1673, Father Jacques Marquette and Louis Jolliet canoed down the Mississippi River. They were the first Europeans to follow the river south to the Arkansas River. Jolliet, an excellent mapmaker, mapped out their travels along the Mississippi River.

Hernando de Soto and his crew encountered many American Indians during their exploration. They stayed in an American Indian village before crossing the Mississippi.

René Robert Cavelier, Sieur de La Salle (1643–1687)

René Robert Cavelier, Sieur de La Salle, was another French explorer who traveled the Mississippi River. French King Louis XIV gave him permission to explore the river down to its mouth. The king also gave him permission to establish forts and trading posts along the way.

La Salle traveled the river by canoe, reaching the Gulf of Mexico in 1682. He claimed the land for France. In honor of his king, La Salle named the area Louisiana.

In 1803, the United States bought the Louisiana Territory from France for $15 million. The sale included more than 820,000 square miles (2.1 million sq. km) of land, along with the Mississippi River. Called the Louisiana Purchase, this sale made the United States one of the largest nations in the world. In 1812, Louisiana became a state.

The Big Picture

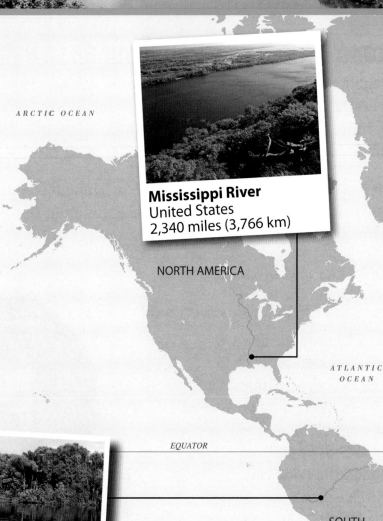

Large rivers are found all over the world. This map shows each continent's major river. Although not shown, even the frozen continent of Antarctica has rivers of ice.

ARCTIC OCEAN

Mississippi River
United States
2,340 miles (3,766 km)

NORTH AMERICA

ATLANTIC OCEAN

EQUATOR

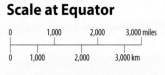

Amazon River
Peru, Brazil
4,000 miles (6,437 km)

PACIFIC OCEAN

SOUTH AMERICA

LEGEND

 Ocean

River

Scale at Equator

0   1,000   2,000   3,000 miles

0   1,000   2,000   3,000 km

N

SOUTHERN OCEAN

Volga River
Russia
2,194 miles (3,531 km)

Yangtze (Chang) River
China
3,900 miles (6,276 km)

ASIA

EUROPE

AFRICA

PACIFIC
OCEAN

EQUATOR

INDIAN
OCEAN

Nile River
Sudan, South Sudan, Burundi,
Rwanda, Democratic Republic
of the Congo, Tanzania, Kenya,
Ethiopia, Uganda, and Egypt
4,160 miles (6,695 km)

AUSTRALIA

Murray River
Australia
1,566 miles (2,520 km)

SOUTHERN
OCEAN

ANTARCTICA

People of the River

People have lived along the Mississippi River for thousands of years. American Indians built communities throughout the area. They fished its waters and hunted birds and animals along its shores. When the river overflowed, rich sediment was left on the **floodplain**, which created soil ideal for farming.

The Ojibwa of northern Minnesota named the river *misi sipi*, which means "great river." The Cherokee, Chickasaw, Choctaw, Creek, and Seminole made their homes in the South. In the early part of the 19th century, the United States Army forced many of these groups to leave their homes and move to an area called Indian Territory, in what is now Oklahoma. Their journey west of the Mississippi River is known as the "Trail of Tears."

Many American Indian groups settled along the banks of the Mississippi River. Besides food, the river provided them with an important transportation route.

Birchbark Canoes

American Indians used birchbark canoes for fishing, for hunting, and to carry goods. These canoes varied in size from about 20 feet (6 m) to 100 feet (30 m) long. The longest canoes required 20 paddlers to move through the water.

American Indians used canoes to travel along the Mississippi River. Canoes were fast and quiet on the water. Many groups in the northeast built a special kind of light, graceful canoe. The canoe's frame was usually white cedar wood. The frame was covered with sheets of bark cut from birch trees. The birchbark sheets were sewn together with spruce tree roots. Then, thick tree sap was rubbed over the canoe to make it waterproof.

Other nations, such as those of the southeast, made dugout canoes. These canoes were created by hollowing out a large tree trunk or log. When European explorers arrived, they saw how useful these American Indian boats were. The Europeans decided to use canoes for traveling the Mississippi River.

Mississippi River Timeline

Prehistoric

5–4 billion years ago Earth is formed.

600–300 million years ago Seas rise and fall over the North American continent.

250 million years ago The course of the Lower Mississippi is established.

1.8–1.5 million years ago Glaciers move forward and then recede.

1.5 million years ago The Upper Mississippi forms.

120,000 years ago The first modern humans evolve.

100,000–75,000 years ago The Wisconsin glacier advances.

12,700 years ago The great Upper Mississippi flood begins.

12,000–10,000 years ago The Wisconsin glacier retreats.

Exploration

1541 Hernando de Soto is the first European to see the Mississippi River.

1673 Father Jacques Marquette and Louis Jolliet canoe down the Mississippi as far as Arkansas.

1682 René Robert Cavelier, Sieur de La Salle, reaches the Gulf of Mexico.

Development

1803 The United States receives the Mississippi River from France as part of the Louisiana Purchase.

1811 The *New Orleans* is the first steamboat to travel the Mississippi River.

1830s–1870s This period is the "golden age" of steamboats.

1861–1865 During the Civil War, the Mississippi River is used by Northern armies to invade the South. It is the scene of many important battles.

1927 The largest flood in the recorded history of the Mississippi River occurs in the lower valley.

1930s Dams with locks are built to deepen the main channel to 9 feet (3 m).

1993 A flood on the Upper Mississippi River causes billions of dollars in damage.

Present

2001 Another large and serious flood happens on the Upper Mississippi.

2011 Extreme flooding causes deaths and property destruction.

2012 The Lower Mississippi experiences a drought that forces an 11-mile (18-km) section of the river to be shut down to shipping traffic.

2012 The force of Hurricane Isaac causes the Mississippi River to flow backwards.

Controlling the Flow

Floods and droughts are important to wildlife habitats along the Mississippi River. However, humans have changed the Mississippi River. Dams, **locks**, and **levees** have been built along the river to control the flow of river water. The Mississippi, with its important role in the water cycle, is in need of protection. By keeping the river healthy, people and wildlife can share and enjoy this wonderful river.

Sixty percent of all grain exported from the United States is transported along the Mississippi River. Locks and dams help maintain a consistent water depth so that ships carrying grain and other goods can travel safely.

Many people believe that the Mississippi River needs to be managed with care. They feel there should be a cooperative effort to clean up the water, restore floodplains, and protect habitats and ecosystems. These efforts include having communities take care of their sections of the river and having state and federal governments work together on dam and flood control projects.

Should humans control the course of the Mississippi River?

Yes	No
Dams and levees created large areas of agricultural land along the river.	Millions of acres (hectares) of wetlands have been drained. This damages the environment and threatens wildlife.
Dams and levees help keep the river from flooding farms, towns, and cities.	Changes in the river's flow mean sediment either settles in the wrong places or is washed away.
Locks make it possible for boats to easily carry cargo up and down the river.	Floods are a natural part of life along the Mississippi River, and dams and levees cannot prevent all of them.

Natural Attractions

The Mississippi River offers visitors many things to see and do. There are wonderful restaurants, festivals, and sporting opportunities, such as fishing.

New Orleans is known for its Creole and Cajun foods. Creole cooking is a delicious mix of African, French, German, Haitian, Italian, American Indian, and Spanish flavors. Cajun cooking often combines meat, seafood, and vegetables. Creole and Cajun food was first developed in Louisiana.

Another popular activity is fishing for catfish. The Mississippi River is full of catfish, named for their long "whiskers."

Every July, the National Tom Sawyer Days are held in Hannibal, Missouri. This festival has delighted visitors since 1956. A fence-painting contest is just one of the many fun festival activities.

Crispy Fried Catfish (serves 6)
Ask a teacher or parent to help you make this delicious Southern dish.

- 6 skinned catfish
- 1/2 cup evaporated milk
- 1 tablespoon salt
- dash of pepper

- 1 cup flour
- 1/2 cup yellow cornmeal
- 2 teaspoons paprika
- 12 slices bacon

Clean, wash, and dry the fish. Combine milk, salt, and pepper in one bowl. Combine flour, cornmeal, and paprika in another bowl. Dip fish in the milk mixture and roll in the flour mixture. Fry bacon in a heavy pan until it is crisp. Remove bacon and drain it on a paper towel. Reserve the fat for frying fish. Fry fish in the hot fat for 4 minutes. Turn the fish over and fry for 4 to 6 minutes longer, or until the fish is brown and flakes easily. Pat the fish with a paper towel.

Source: The Mississippi Cookbook

Paddle Steamers

In the summer of 1870, the *Natchez* and *Robert E. Lee* steamboats competed in a famous three-day race along the Mississippi from New Orleans to St. Louis. A modern replica of the *Natchez* is still operating river cruises today.

"Steamboat's a-comin'!" At one time, this excited cry could be heard up and down the Mississippi River. Steamboats, or paddle steamers, ruled the river. These long, tall boats carried people and cargo. Wood fires heated the huge boilers. The boilers, in turn, produced steam, moving the great paddle wheels.

The first steamboat to travel down the Mississippi River was the *New Orleans*. It set sail in 1811. By the 1850s, more than 3,000 paddle steamers were docking at the port of New Orleans. Today, the *Delta Queen* continues to offer visitors a chance to cruise the Mississippi River on a traditional paddle steamer. This beautiful steamboat is a National Historic Landmark.

River Stories

The Mississippi River has inspired many writers. Mark Twain's stories are the best known. Twain grew up in Hannibal, Missouri, a town along the Mississippi River. Mark Twain loved the river and wrote about it in many of his books. He thought the Mississippi River had "a new story to tell every day."

In 1876, Twain published *The Adventures of Tom Sawyer*. In 1884, Twain wrote *The Adventures of Huckleberry Finn*, which has come to be his most popular book. Some of the most exciting events in *The Adventures of Huckleberry Finn* take place on the Mississippi River. Huck and his friend Jim escape capture by sailing down the river on a raft. Both of these books are still popular today.

Mark Twain's book *The Adventures of Tom Sawyer* is about the adventures of a boy growing up alongside the Mississippi River.

Mississippi Music

African Americans living in the Mississippi Delta developed a type of music called the blues. They based this music on work songs and spirituals created by African Americans who had been made to work as slaves. The blues are usually slow, moody songs with a strong rhythm. The songs communicate African-American experiences.

Another type of music, known as jazz, developed out of the blues. Jazz became popular in the early 1900s in the city of New Orleans, Louisiana. People still travel to New Orleans to hear the many excellent jazz bands.

Many people associate the saxophone with jazz music, but the first jazz bands in New Orleans actually used trumpets or cornets as the lead instrument.

True or False?

Decide whether the following statements are true or false. If the statement is false, make it true.

1. About 100 species of wildlife live in or on the Mississippi River.

2. Creole and Cajun cooking developed in Minnesota.

3. The Mississippi River begins as a tiny stream.

4. Hernando de Soto gave Louisiana its name.

5. Travelers can still ride on the Delta Queen.

6. Cotton is grown in the Mississippi Delta.

ANSWERS
1. False. About 400 species of wildlife live on or in the Mississippi River.
2. False. Creole and Cajun cooking developed in Louisiana.
3. True.
4. False. René Cavelier, Sieur de La Salle, named Louisiana.
5. True.
6. True.

Short Answer

Answer the following questions using information from the book.

1. What are the three sections of the Mississippi River?
2. In the water cycle, where does fresh water come from?
3. Who wrote *The Adventures of Tom Sawyer*?
4. In which year did La Salle reach the mouth of the Mississippi River?
5. What are three types of human structures that help control the Mississippi River?

Multiple Choice

Choose the best answer for the following questions.

1. Jazz developed out of what type of music?
   a. rap
   b. rock
   c. blues

2. American Indians built what kind of boat for traveling the river?
   a. steamboat
   b. canoe
   c. rowboat

3. "Mississippi" comes from Ojibwa, meaning what?
   a. "long water"
   b. "great river"
   c. "river of mud"

4. In prehistoric times, what helped carve out the Mississippi River?
   a. glaciers
   b. tidal waves
   c. floods

Activity

Glacier Movement

Glaciers took a long time to carve their way through North America. One way that glaciers move is called creeping. As snow falls, more **mass** is added to the top of the glacier. This layer becomes so heavy that it flattens deeper layers of snow, forming packed ice. The solid layers of ice slide over each other and push outward. The glacier creeps more with each snowfall. Do this experiment to see how glaciers creep.

Materials

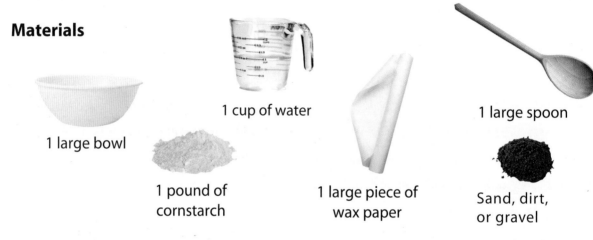

1 large bowl

1 cup of water

1 pound of cornstarch

1 large piece of wax paper

1 large spoon

Sand, dirt, or gravel

Instructions

1. Put the cornstarch and water in the bowl, and mix them together.

2. Using the spoon, place one large scoop of the cornstarch mixture in the middle of the paper. This is the first part of your glacier.

3. Pour a small amount of the mixture on top of the last dollop. This is new snowfall. Notice how the lower layer spreads out under the weight of the addition.

4. Spread a thin half-circle of sand, dirt, or gravel near your glacier.

5. Keep adding the mixture until the glacier reaches the half-circle of gravel. What happens to the gravel? Continue adding spoonfuls until the glacier almost reaches the edge of the wax paper. This is quite similar to how a real glacier moves and grows.

Key Words

basin: the region draining into a river

delta: a large, triangle-shaped area at the mouth of a river

ecosystem: a community of plants, animals, and their environment

floodplain: low, flat land that is flooded by a river

glaciers: large masses of moving ice

headwaters: the source or water near the source of a river

levees: riverbanks built by people to prevent flooding

locks: gates closing off part of a river

mass: the quantity of matter that a body contains

refuge: a protected area

sediment: mud, sand, and pieces of rock that are moved by water

species: a specific group of plant or animal that shares characteristics

tributaries: streams that flow into a river

water cycle: circular movement of water through ground and sky

wetlands: low, wet wildlife habitat area, such as a marsh or swamp

Index

Log on to www.av2books.com

AV² by Weigl brings you media enhanced books that support active learning. Go to www.av2books.com, and enter the special code found on page 2 of this book. You will gain access to enriched and enhanced content that supplements and complements this book. Content includes video, audio, weblinks, quizzes, a slide show, and activities.

AV² Online Navigation

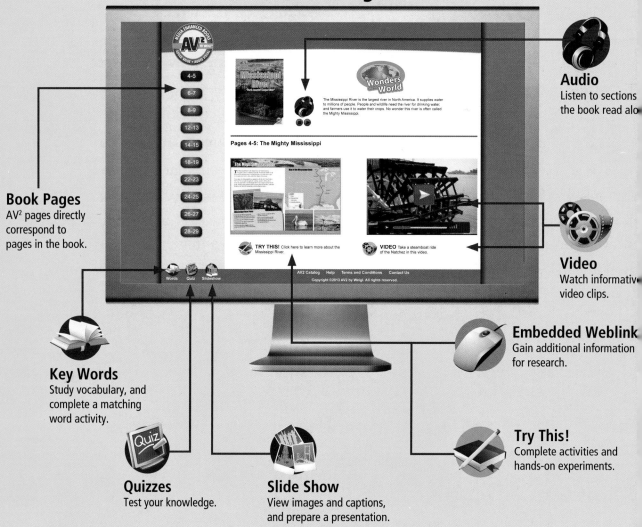

Audio
Listen to sections the book read alo

Book Pages
AV² pages directly correspond to pages in the book.

Video
Watch informativ
video clips.

Key Words
Study vocabulary, and complete a matching word activity.

Embedded Weblink
Gain additional information for research.

Try This!
Complete activities and hands-on experiments.

Quizzes
Test your knowledge.

Slide Show
View images and captions, and prepare a presentation.

AV² was built to bridge the gap between print and digital. We encourage you to tell us what you like and what you want to see in the future.

Sign up to be an AV² Ambassador at www.av2books.com/ambassador.